MURAT MEMALLAJ

AF430926

Nocturnal Muses

Nocturnal Muses

(an andonmanajbooks.com production)

Contents

PREFACE:

Armed with the ability to create lines after lines of poetry and getting inspired from the smallest things that surround him, Mr. Memallaj is a unique artist. That small stature of a man, has the power to hold Your entire World in the palm of his hand. Him and him alone can lift you up when you're feeling down and dry your tears when you're feeling sad. As an author of too many short stories myself, I find it really hard to describe the magical world in which Mr. Memallaj immerses you through his ways of poetry.

Andon Manaj

EDITOR

The introduction looks like a construction.
When there is no introduction,
There is no creation,
There is no connection,
There is no relation…

"Hello!"

This word looks like a light!

And when We use "Goodmorning!"

"Good day! Good night!"

And then you ask: "How are you?"

My answer is: "I am fine! Thank you!"

If your mood is bad,

Have bad news,

I ask: "What's up?"

"What's about you?"

Oh – how beautiful would have been this world!

If we so loved each – other!

And appreciate everybody

When you say: "How are you my sister?"

"How are you my brother?"

You have gone very early,

    Though you lived very long!

You have rebirthed in many humans,

    By your beautiful song…

A song that calls to everyone,

    Calls also to me…

Wake up! Wake up my friend,

    If you want to be free!

You say: they say that life is a highway

    And it's milestones are years…

And now and then there is a toll-gate,

    Where you pay your way with your tears…

It's a rough road; steep road,

    And it stretches broad and far…

But at least it leads to a Golden Town,

    Where the Golden Houses are….

BODY LANGUAGE

I think that everyone is a psychiatrist,

    Even though they don't study psychology…

Everybody is able to understand,

    When someone is busy and free…

Everybody is able to know,

    When someone is poor or rich…

Enough to see their view,

    In their body language…

I think that everybody is able to know,

    When someone is a crow and a dove…

When your eyes are telling you,

    When you're with someone you hate or love…

I SWEAR....

I swear that I shall never forget your face,

I never forget your view,

Whether the sky will be very gray,

Whether the sky will be very blue…

There is a reason for everything,

And for what I would like to say it's true.

I shall never forget that moment,

When you said: I have been looking for so long for you..

I vow that I shall never forget your sweet voice,

I shall never forget your word,

I swear that it is the best feeling,

That I have ever felt in this world!

COFFEE I

I'd like to drink coffee,

A coffee made by me,

Because I am very tired,

And I'd like to be free.

Coffee is very good,

For your heart ,

And for the brain,

When you drink coffee,

You have erased the pain.

TRIBUTE TO BRITISH AIRWAYS

Why are you very happy?!

And your mood is so good?

-Oh, is it the BA "bread"?

Or is it the BA food?

-Wow!

Your response is a miracle!

Your response is beautiful!

I never forget this reply,

It is very meaningful!

-It's a beautiful pleasure,

To travel with BA!

To go to United Kingdom,

And to come through this way!

To look at the agent's smile,

And their wishes as light,

Have a nice trip!

Have a nice day!

And

Enjoy your nice flight!

LISTEN.... LEARN...

Do you want to talk?

Listen to learn!

Listen to learn,

And learn to listen,

Is a great way,

So only learn to listen

And only listen to learn,

You will be okay!

In this world you are different,

Love those who hit you…

With words!

Your revenge is your improvement.

That means you've got talent!

ENCHANTED THOUGHTS

Your black hair took my view,

On the moment I was with you,

Your black long strands of hair are the best,

Their two branches – on your chest.

And those hair strands that are all black,

Are covering sweetly all your back!

Your face is white,

Is all white..

Your glasses give you a sweet light!

You look nice! Very nice!

You are healing those desires,

It is nice to see you like a sun ray…

I appreciate you

      For this good day!

LONELINES

When I have been lonely,

Like an orphan in a foreign land,

A lady send to me a smile,

That stays in my mind for a long time – alive.

The lady asked me: "Where are you from?"

"I am Albanian – country man from Tepelena."

She told me 'I am from Austria."

But for you is very well-known Vienna.

There is George Kastriot's sword,

So well known in this world.

JEALOUSY

I am not jealous with everybody,

I am not jealous with God,

That created this world…

I am not jealous with someone that invented the nail,

And the sword…

I am jealous with someone that invented the wheel.

This is one of the first inventions in this world,

The one that is not ignored to this day – still…

Before to tell someone

    "I am sorry!"

You must tell yourself

    "Be careful!"

This is an imperative,

But this is more meaningful…

It is much better to be happy…

    It is not better to be rude…

Our life looks like a lady,

    But one minute is very good…

I would like to be with you,

I would like with you a hike,

I would like to talk for you,

I would like your smile,

Your like…

Love yourself!

    Take care of yourself!

        This advise is true!

"Push yourself" – tells us a saying,

    "Because nobody else can do it,

            for you…'

MY JOB

I love my job,

    I am trying to be very good at it,

Be cause without a job…

    I can not eat

        I cannot eat bread

            I cannot eat meat.

I like Robert De Niro's advice

    And I always remind myself to it:

"Go out and earn it,

So no one can say

They gave you shit!"

Love yourself!

    Take care of yourself!

        As yourself you cannot find.

Love your body,

    Like your eyes!

        Love and improve your mind!

Love yourself and love your family,

    Love your daughters and your sons!

But you can't forget honey of honey..

    Like granddaughters and grandsons!

Love your mother and your father,

    Love your sisters and your brothers!

This world has enough words,

    And each words have self value..

But more expansive in this world,

    Naturally is "I love You!"

Love your friend and love your love…

    Don't forget either one..

When you wish good luck to your friends..

Your life will be very fun!

COFFEE II

I'd like to have a coffee,

    A coffee that is made by you,

Because I am very tired,

What would you think?

    Is it true?

\-   A coffee is very good,

      For your brain and for your heart

Some say that the best coffee…

    Is only at Dunkin' Donuts!

When everyone has no success in their lives,

When everyone has no good luck…

From their tongues explode three really sweet words…

"Oh my God.. Oh Shit… Oh Fu…"

I want to ask my favorite poet..

    I would like to communicate with you,

                Robert Frost..

Can you tell me,

    What does hate means?

Can you tell me,

    What does it cost in this world?

Some say life is good,

    Some say life is nice,

Somewhere you wrote:

    "the world will end in fire"

        And somewhere "in ice."

I would like to know,

    What'd happen if the world would perish twice?

My answer will be the same,

    "I think I know enough of hate,"

To say that for the destruction,

    Ice is also great,

        And would suffice…

Manager Ali,

    Manager Ali,

You have good luck working with me..

    Working with me,

        You can buy iPhone!

But you'll be homeless…

    Working with Solomon.

One day god

    Told to JetBlue,

        "Do you believe in me?"

JetBlue said: "No!"

    "Okay then," God said…

"Today you're off,

`   Cause I'll drop some snow"

And then all flights are cancelled,

    And God said: "Let's go!"

"No, I believe in you," – said JetBlue…

    "I don't like to fly under the snow…"

Then God asked the crew:

    "Which weather is better for you?"

"Naturally," – came a sweet voice,

    "When the sky is very blue!"

I wish good luck to everyone,

    I wish good luck to every crew,

You can fly with every airline,

    But you jet better with JetBlue!

I know someone may dislike this poem,

Naturally, dislike every crew,

But I have heard God himself say:

"I've never seen better then JetBlue!

One day I had a quarrel with god,

    I told him my pain…

        "Why have you brought me in this world?

            Where I am suffering from my brain?"

He told me,

    "Take it easy my son,

        Because the world is big,

            And life for you is done!"

"I have brought you in this world,

    For you to know,

        For you to change,

            To feel pleasure….

                And the pain…

And then…

    When you have improved the world's brain,

        You don't like to come with me again…"

I told him,

    "I like change!

        I have changed the continent,

    But I would like to change the planet!"

His answer was very short,

"Not yet, my son…

Not yet….."

Not everyone can write verses for you,

    No everyone can sculpt your portrait,

Not everyone can love you like I do,

    Only one like me,

        Can never forget!

MUSE PART I

It's much better to be happy,

Our life looks like a flower,

But to live this life, my friend,

Naturally, you need the power!

It's more better to be happy,

It's no better to be rude,

Our life looks like a flower,

Keeps blooming every season!

Sometimes the weather is dark,

And sometimes is bright,

Sometimes the life is good,

And sometimes hasn't light.

Sometimes someone is very good,

And sometimes very rude,

Sometimes the life is a lie,

And sometimes life is the truth,

Sometimes someone says: I can't!

But you always say: I can do!

SHUT UP!

To tell someone: Shut up!

Naturally, is a rude way.

It is to tell him: Get out!

And attention don't pay

But, if you tell me: Shut up!

I feel myself free,

Because you're not able to listen,

And to communicate with me.

To hear someone is a good gift,

So don't give up!

It is good to be patient and never say: Shut up!

FOREVER

If you want to live forever,

To live long and very long,

Allow me to see your body,

And to write for you a song,

And my song will live forever,

As long as the lives of Gods,

And you will be – will be forever,

Like a flower,

Like a bud!

If you want to live forever,

To live long and to be free,

Please read Percy B. Shelley,

And learn Love's Philosophy,

You have read many poets…

But who is best?

Who is he?

He is Percy B. Shelley

That knows Love's Philosophy,

Nothing in the world is single,

All things by a law divine…

In one spirit meet and mingle,

Why not I with Thine?

Why I love so much?

And only for you I cry?

Are you a sweet girl?

Are you a butterfly?

Yes – I am a sweet coffee!

Without sugar and cream,

I am your life – your sun,

I am your dream…

I have never been in China,

But I know how Chinese are,

Today I have seen a girl from China,

She was far from us, so far…

She was a wonderful girl!

And she needs a podium,

I have a poetic license,

And for her I wrote a poem!

DON'T CRY!

Will come a day and all will die,
And you, and them, and I.
And everybody will rot in hell,
And nobody in the sky!

And this is true.
Believe to me,
Because I don't like to lie.

When you'll finish crying,
Please let your tears dry,
And always: See later,
And never say: Goodbye!

Murat Memallaj was born in the small antiquated town of
Tepelena, Albania. His inspiration to create lines of poetry
stemmed from his work as a literature teacher in the
town's middle school. This days Murat resides in Revere,
Massachusetts with his wife. He enjoys taking walks by
the boardwalk: with each step a new line is born.

www.ingramcontent.com/pod-product-compliance
Lightning Source LLC
Chambersburg PA
CBHW031134160726
47989CB00017B/2974